UNDER MY NOSE

by

Lois Ehlert

photographs by

Carlo Ontal

Richard C. Owen Publishers, Inc.
Katonah, New York

Meet the Author titles

Verna Aardema *A Bookworm Who Hatched*
Frank Asch *One Man Show*
Eve Bunting *Once Upon a Time*
Lois Ehlert *Under My Nose*
Jean Fritz *Surprising Myself*
Paul Goble *Hau Kola Hello Friend*
Ruth Heller *Fine Lines*
Lee Bennett Hopkins *The Writing Bug*
James Howe *Playing with Words*

Karla Kuskin *Thoughts, Pictures, and Words*
George Ella Lyon *A Wordful Child*
Margaret Mahy *My Mysterious World*
Rafe Martin *A Storyteller's Story*
Patricia McKissack *Can You Imagine?*
Patricia Polacco *Firetalking*
Laurence Pringle *Nature! Wild and Wonderful*
Cynthia Rylant *Best Wishes*
Jane Yolen *A Letter from Phoenix Farm*

Text copyright © 1996 by Lois Ehlert
Photographs copyright © 1996 by Carlo Ontal

Richard C. Owen Publishers, Inc.
PO Box 585
Katonah, New York 10536

Library of Congress Cataloging-in-Publication Data

Ehlert , Lois .
      Under my nose / by Lois Ehlert ; photographs by Carlo Ontal .
      p .   cm . — (Meet the author)
      Summary: Author and illustrator of books for young people , Lois
Ehlert , shares how she interweaves her creative process with her daily routine.
      ISBN 1-57274-027-2
      1 . Ehlert, Lois — Biography — Juvenile literature . 2 . Women
authors , American — 20th century — Biography — Juvenile literature .
3 . Women Illustrators — United States — Biography — Juvenile
literature . 4 . Children's literature — Authorship — Juvenile
literature . 5 . Illustration of books — Juvenile literature .
[1 . Ehlert , Lois .   2 . Authors , American . 3 . Illustrators .
4 . Women — Biography .]   I . Title . II . Series : Meet the author
(Katonah , N . Y .)
PS3555.H55Z477   1996
813' .54—dc20
[B]
                                                            96 - 15441
                                                                  CIP
                                                                   AC

Editorial, Art, and Production Director   *Janice Boland*
Production Assistant   *Matthew Vartabedian*
Color separations by Leo P. Callahan Inc., Binghamton, NY

Printed in the United States of America

9 8 7 6 5 4 3 2

To my family, with thanks and love

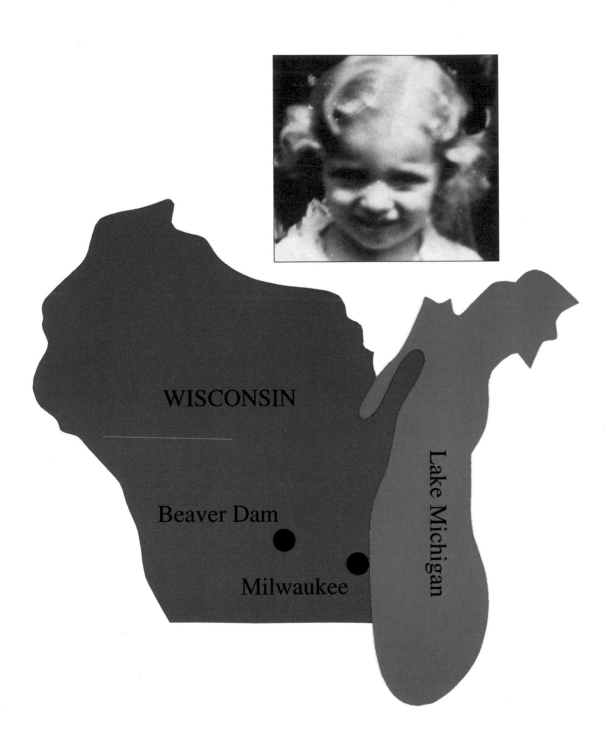

WISCONSIN

Beaver Dam

Milwaukee

Lake Michigan

I grew up in this house in Beaver Dam, Wisconsin.
My mother still lives here.

I'm the oldest of three children.
I have a sister and a brother.
Their children have spent many happy hours
working with me in my studio.

My nephew drew this picture of me.

I can't recall when I first wanted
to create children's books.
But I always read a lot of books.
Now I have tons of books at home,
books in every room, but I still go to libraries.

I go to bookstores too,
to look at books and buy
more books.

By the time I was in high school,

I knew I wanted to be an artist.

I didn't know any artists.

I never took an art class.

I drew and painted on my own.

My inner feelings about art were very strong.

After graduating from high school,

I spent four years in art school. It was heaven!

I carried a sketch pad to draw on

and a note pad to describe in words

what I saw with my eyes.

That must have been the beginning of my writing.

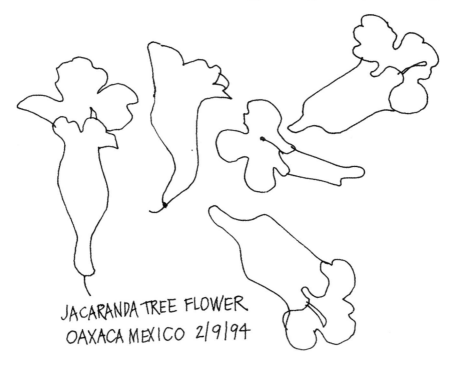

JACARANDA TREE FLOWER
OAXACA MEXICO 2/9/94

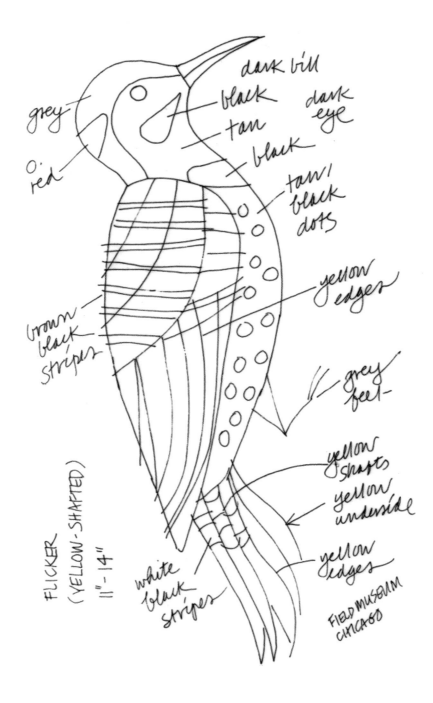

grey

o
red

dark bill

black

tan

black

dark
eye

tan/
black
dots

yellow
edges

brown
black
stripes

grey
feet

FLICKER
(YELLOW-SHAFTED)
11" - 14"

yellow
shafts

yellow
underside

yellow
edges

white
black
stripes

FIELD MUSEUM
CHICAGO

11

When I began my career, I designed
and illustrated books written by other authors.
When you illustrate a book, this is how it works.
After a publisher buys an author's manuscript,
the editor and the art director choose an artist
to illustrate the story. As an artist, my job
after reading the manuscript is to decide
if I want to illustrate the book, and how I will do it.

When I read *Chicka Chicka Boom Boom*,
I liked the beat of the words
and decided to draw the letters
as if they were dancing to music.
Several years after I had completed the
illustrations, I met the authors, Bill Martin, Jr.
and John Archambault, at a book conference.
I was nervous. Did they like the way I illustrated
their story? Lucky for me they did.

Before I began the artwork for *Crocodile Smile*
I listened to a tape of Sarah Weeks, the author/
composer, singing the words to her songs.

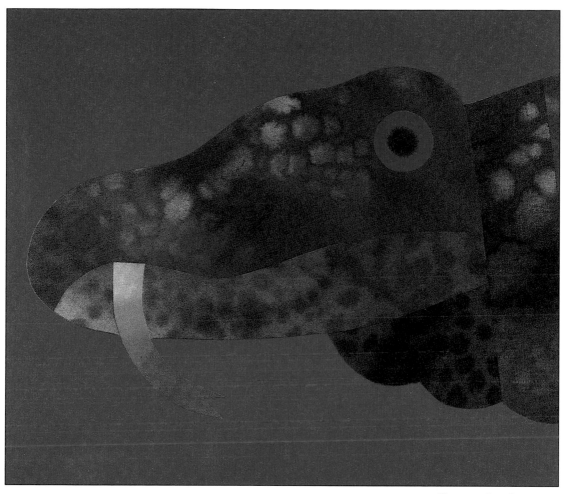

Komodo dragon

I loved the music and words and decided to paint
a watercolor portrait of each animal, choosing
colors that would match the mood of each song.
I even designed the box with the smiling crocodile
to keep the tape and book together.

I never planned to be a writer,
but something happened
that changed my mind.
About ten years ago I took a
course to learn how to make
handmade books. The books
I made needed text, so I began
writing words to go with my art.
About the same time, I had an
idea for a story about my garden.

Some friends and I
shared a vegetable
garden at the edge of
the city of Milwaukee.
I knew I could write
about the vegetables
and make sketches of
them on the spot.
They were right under
my nose.

Three years later, my book *Growing Vegetable Soup*
was published. It was the first book I illustrated
and wrote.

Getting a good idea for a book
is the hardest thing for me,
but also the most fun.
Watching Milwaukee's annual circus parade
with its flashy colors and interesting animals
inspired the idea for my book *Circus*
and these marching snakes.

Living close to Lake Michigan, I like to take long walks. One day while I was outside, a squirrel slipped inside my house through a torn window screen. That gave me the idea for a book. In *Nuts to You!* I tell how I got him out.

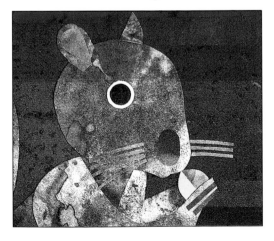

When I write my books, I start with the
picture first. Bucky, my sister's cat, was my
model for *Feathers for Lunch*. Before I wrote
the story I measured his legs, his head, and
his tail, and painted a life-sized portrait of
him. The story is about a cat trying to catch
a bird. That's why I put the bell on his
collar—it warns the birds. I added the words
"jingle, jingle" to go with my art.

I began writing the story from the cat's viewpoint.
Later, I rewrote it from the cat owner's viewpoint.

cat's viewpoint
↓

Door's left open,
just a crack.

Going out,
might not be back!

Food in a can
is not too exciting;

when there are things
I'd rather be biting.

cat owner's
viewpoint
↓

Oh, oh.
Door's left open,
just a crack,

My cat is out,
and he won't come back!

His food in a can
is tame and mild,
so he's gone out
for something wild,

Even when I get an idea for a book,
it's difficult for me to get started.

SLEEK
SLIPPERY
STRIPED
SPOTTED
WIGGLE
SMOOTH
SQUISHY
FLAT
CHUBBY
SLICK
FLUTTER
SWIMMING
FLASHY
GLITTER
SLENDER
SHORT
GLIDING
FLIPPING
SPLASHY
JUMPING
BEAUTIFUL

Once I wanted to do a book about fish. I even had a title, *Fish Eyes*. To get myself in the mood, I made a list of fishy words. I wondered how it would feel to swim like a fish. Could I put those feelings into words and pictures? I went to the aquarium and made sketches as I watched beautiful fish swim by. I read so much about fish that I felt fish would swim out of my ears.

Look for me. I tell a story too.

I like to write out rough story ideas for my books,
then make thumbnail sketches. These are from
Feathers for Lunch.

and
some
orange
flowers,

tulip

Next, I make the dummy book.
I sketch in the art and hand-letter the words.
These are pages from the dummy book I made
for *Planting a Rainbow*. I go over my dummy book
with my editor. I like to read the text out loud
and listen to the rhythm of the words. The text
and the art should help each other tell the story.

POPPY

I type the text on my typewriter in my sunroom, where I'm surrounded by flowers, books, and plants. It's quiet and peaceful here, just the way I like it when I'm writing.

For my illustrations, I cut paper or material and glue the pieces to background paper. It's the kind of thing I liked to do when I was growing up. The art technique is called collage. I used plain colored paper for *Circus*, *Color Zoo*, and *Color Farm*. For *Red Leaf*, *Yellow Leaf* and *Snowballs* I painted with watercolors and glued down real objects. I cut and glued forty-three pieces of paper to make the pineapple for *Eating the Alphabet*.

P p

PINEAPPLE
pineapple

PEACH
peach

PEAR
pear

When book ideas just won't come, I stare out the
window, water my plants, or go for a walk.
I believe ideas need fresh air, too.

I might wash my car, visit my mother, listen to the
radio and sing along, find another antique charm
for my vest, or just sit and read.

Then I sharpen my pencils and it's back to work I go, trying to get those words and pictures to tell a story.

As I go along, I continue to learn more about art and writing. If you like to write and draw, I hope you will keep learning, too. Good luck and keep your eyes open. There might be a story right under your nose.

Lois Ehlert

Other Books by Lois Ehlert

Color Zoo; Color Farm; Feathers for Lunch; Red Leaf, Yellow Leaf; Snowballs

About the Photographer

Carlo Ontal traveled from Minnesota to Wisconsin to spend several days with Lois Ehlert taking the pictures for this book. Carlo also took the photographs for Cynthia Rylant's Meet the Author book, *Best Wishes*.

Acknowledgments

Photographs on pages 4, 5, 6, and 20 courtesy of Lois Ehlert. Map on page 4 by Lois Ehlert. Portrait on page 7 by James Dinsch courtesy of Lois Ehlert. Illustrations on pages 10 and 11 by Lois Ehlert courtesy of Lois Ehlert. Illustration on page 13 from *Chicka Chicka Boom Boom* by Bill Martin, Jr. and John Archambault, illustrated by Lois Ehlert. Illustrations copyright 1989 by Lois Ehlert. Reprinted with permission of Simon & Schuster Books for Young Readers. Illustration on page 15 from *Crocodile Smile: Ten Songs of the Earth as the Animals See It*, Read Along Book written and sung by Sarah Weeks, illustrated by Lois Ehlert. Illustrations copyright 1994 by Lois Ehlert. Reprinted with permission of HarperCollins Publishers. Illustrations on pages 16 and 17 from *Growing Vegetable Soup* written and illustrated by Lois Ehlert. Copyright 1987 by Lois Ehlert. Reprinted with permission of Harcourt Brace & Company. Illustration on page 18 courtesy of Lois Ehlert from *Circus* by Lois Ehlert. Copyright 1992 by Lois Ehlert. Selection reprinted with permission of HarperCollins Publishers. Illustration on page 19 from *Nuts to You!* by Lois Ehlert. Copyright 1993 by Lois Ehlert. Published by Harcourt Brace Jovanovich. Reprinted with permission of Harcourt Brace & Company. Illustration on page 23 from *Fish Eyes* by Lois Ehlert. Copyright 1990 by Lois Ehlert. Published by Harcourt Brace Jovanovich. Reprinted with permission of Harcourt Brace & Company. Thumbnail sketches on pages 24 and 25 courtesy of Lois Ehlert. Illustrations on pages 26 and 27 from *Planting a Rainbow* by Lois Ehlert. Copyright 1988 by Lois Ehlert. Published by Harcourt Brace Jovanovich Publishers. Reprinted with permission of Harcourt Brace & Company. Illustration on page 28 from *Eating the Alphabet* by Lois Ehlert. Copyright 1989 by Lois Ehlert. Published by Harcourt Brace Jovanovich Publishers. Reprinted with permission of Harcourt Brace & Company.